Flute

101 MOST BEAUTIFUL SONGS

Available for
FLUTE, CLARINET, ALTO SAX, TENOR SAX, TRUMPET,
HORN, TROMBONE, VIOLIN, VIOLA, CELLO

ISBN 978-1-5400-4812-7

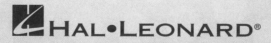

Visit Hal Leonard Online at
www.halleonard.com

World headquarters, contact:
Hal Leonard
7777 West Bluemound Road
Milwaukee, WI 53213
Email: info@halleonard.com

In Europe, contact:
Hal Leonard Europe Limited
1 Red Place
London, W1K 6PL
Email: info@halleonardeurope.com

In Australia, contact:
Hal Leonard Australia Pty. Ltd.
4 Lentara Court
Cheltenham, Victoria, 3192 Australia
Email: info@halleonard.com.au

CONTENTS

ALWAYS

FLUTE

Words and Music by
IRVING BERLIN

ALWAYS ON MY MIND

Flute

Words and Music by WAYNE THOMPSON,
MARK JAMES and JOHNNY CHRISTOPHER

AND I LOVE HER

Flute

Words and Music by JOHN LENNON
and PAUL McCARTNEY

AND I LOVE YOU SO

Flute

Words and Music by
DON McLEAN

AND SO IT GOES

FLUTE

Words and Music by
BILLY JOEL

Slow Ballad, with much rubato

ANNIE'S SONG

Flute

Words and Music by
JOHN DENVER

ANYWHERE IS

Words and Music by ENYA,
NICKY RYAN and ROMA RYAN

Flute

BEIN' GREEN

FLUTE

Words and Music by
JOE RAPOSO

BLACKBIRD

FLUTE

Words and Music by JOHN LENNON
and PAUL McCARTNEY

THE BOOK OF LOVE

FLUTE

Words and Music by
STEPHIN MERRITT

THE BOXER

FLUTE

Words and Music by
PAUL SIMON

Moderately, in 2

BRING HIM HOME
from LES MISÉRABLES

Flute

Music by CLAUDE-MICHEL SCHÖNBERG
Lyrics by HERBERT KRETZMER and ALAIN BOUBLIL

BY THE TIME I GET TO PHOENIX

FLUTE

Words and Music by
JIMMY WEBB

CANDLE IN THE WIND

Flute

Words and Music by ELTON JOHN
and BERNIE TAUPIN

A CHILD IS BORN

FLUTE

By THAD JONES

(They Long to Be)
CLOSE TO YOU

Flute

Lyrics by HAL DAVID
Music by BURT BACHARACH

CITY OF STARS
from LA LA LAND

Flute

Music by JUSTIN HURWITZ
Lyrics by BENJ PASEK & JUSTIN PAUL

COME SUNDAY
from BLACK, BROWN & BEIGE

FLUTE

By DUKE ELLINGTON

CRAZY

FLUTE

Words and Music by
WILLIE NELSON

CRYING

FLUTE

Words and Music by ROY ORBISON
and JOE MELSON

DREAM A LITTLE DREAM OF ME

Flute

Words by GUS KAHN
Music by WILBUR SCHWANDT
and FABIAN ANDREE

DAUGHTERS

Flute

Words and Music by
JOHN MAYER

D.S. al Coda

CODA

EASY LIVING
Theme from the Paramount Picture EASY LIVING

Flute

Words and Music by LEO ROBIN
and RALPH RAINGER

ETERNAL FLAME

Flute

Words and Music by BILLY STEINBERG,
TOM KELLY and SUSANNA HOFFS

ETERNALLY

FLUTE

Words by GEOFFREY PARSONS
Music by CHARLES CHAPLIN

Slowly, with feeling

EVERY BREATH YOU TAKE

FLUTE

Music and Lyrics by
STING

(EVERYTHING I DO) I DO IT FOR YOU

from the Motion Picture ROBIN HOOD: PRINCE OF THIEVES

FLUTE

Written by MICHAEL KAMEN

FEELING GOOD

from THE ROAR OF THE GREASEPAINT – THE SMELL OF THE CROWD

Flute

Words and Music by LESLIE BRICUSSE
and ANTHONY NEWLEY

FOR ALL WE KNOW

Flute

Words by SAM M. LEWIS
Music by J. FRED COOTS

GABRIEL'S OBOE

from the Motion Picture THE MISSION

Flute

Words and Music by
ENNIO MORRICONE

Slowly, expressively

GOOD NIGHT

FLUTE

Words and Music by JOHN LENNON
and PAUL McCARTNEY

GOODNIGHT, SWEETHEART, GOODNIGHT
(Goodnight, It's Time to Go)

Flute

Words and Music by JAMES HUDSON
and CALVIN CARTER

HAVE I TOLD YOU LATELY

FLUTE

Words and Music by
VAN MORRISON

HELLO

FLUTE

Words and Music by
LIONEL RICHIE

HEAL THE WORLD

FLUTE

Words and Music by
MICHAEL JACKSON

(small notes optional)

CODA

D.S. al Coda

HERE, THERE AND EVERYWHERE

FLUTE

Words and Music by JOHN LENNON
and PAUL McCARTNEY

HIGHLAND CATHEDRAL

Flute

By MICHAEL KORB
and ULRICH ROEVER

Stately March, in 2

I HAVE A DREAM

from MAMMA MIA!

Flute

Words and Music by BENNY ANDERSSON
and BJÖRN ULVAEUS

D.S. al Coda

CODA

I LEFT MY HEART IN SAN FRANCISCO

Flute

Words by DOUGLASS CROSS
Music by GEORGE CORY

I WILL

FLUTE

Words and Music by JOHN LENNON
and PAUL McCARTNEY

I'LL BE AROUND

Flute

Words and Music by
ALEC WILDER

I'LL BE SEEING YOU

from RIGHT THIS WAY

Flute

Written by IRVING KAHAL
and SAMMY FAIN

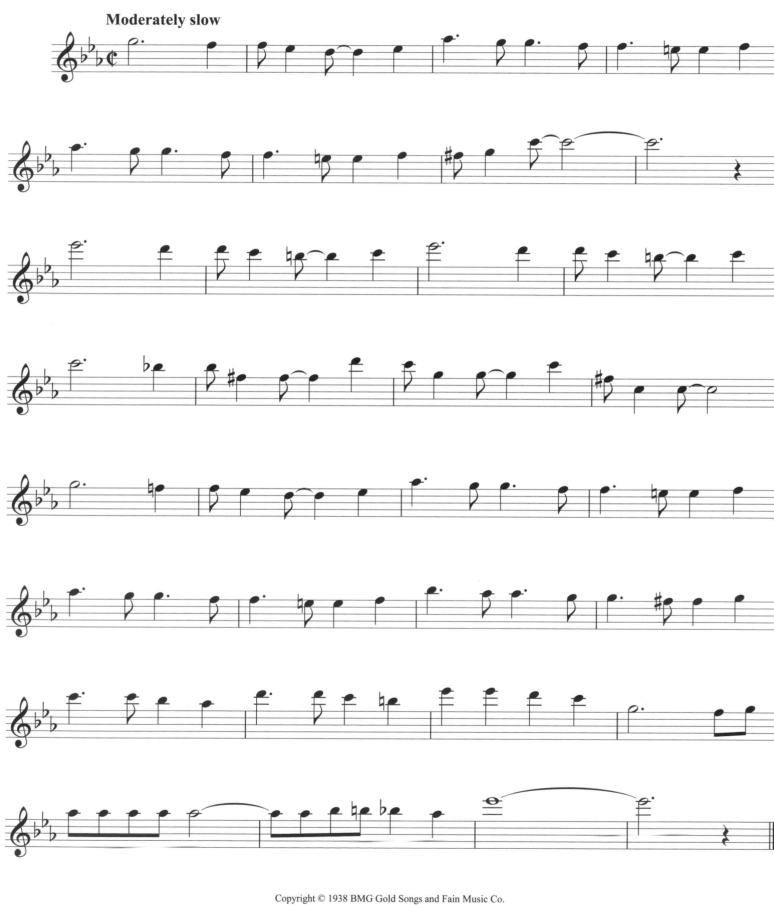

I'VE DREAMED OF YOU

Flute

Words and Music by ANN HAMPTON CALLAWAY
and ROLF LOVLAND

IN MY ROOM

Flute

Words and Music by BRIAN WILSON
and GARY USHER

LA VIE EN ROSE
(Take Me to Your Heart Again)

Flute

Original French Lyrics by EDITH PIAF
Music by LUIGUY
English Lyrics by MACK DAVID

JUST GIVE ME A REASON

FLUTE

Words and Music by ALECIA MOORE,
JEFF BHASKER and NATE RUESS

CODA

LADY IN RED

FLUTE

Words and Music by
CHRIS DeBURGH

LET IT BE ME
(Je t'appartiens)

Flute

English Words by MANN CURTIS
French Words by PIERRE DeLANOE
Music by GILBERT BECAUD

LOST IN YOUR EYES

FLUTE

Words and Music by
DEBORAH GIBSON

Moderately slow

61

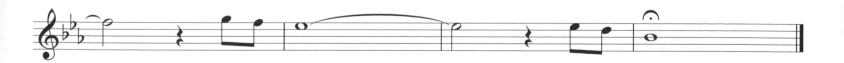

LOVE ME TENDER

FLUTE

Words and Music by ELVIS PRESLEY
and VERA MATSON

LOVING YOU

Flute

Words and Music by JERRY LEIBER
and MIKE STOLLER

LULLABYE
(Goodnight, My Angel)

FLUTE

Words and Music by
BILLY JOEL

Rubato, gently

MIA & SEBASTIAN'S THEME

from LA LA LAND

FLUTE

Music by
JUSTIN HURWITZ

MICHELLE

Flute

Words and Music by JOHN LENNON
and PAUL McCARTNEY

MONA LISA

from the Paramount Picture CAPTAIN CAREY, U.S.A.

Flute

Words and Music by JAY LIVINGSTON
and RAY EVANS

MY FOOLISH HEART

FLUTE

Words by NED WASHINGTON
Music by VICTOR YOUNG

MY FUNNY VALENTINE

from BABES IN ARMS

Flute

Words by LORENZ HART
Music by RICHARD RODGERS

MY VALENTINE

FLUTE

Words and Music by
PAUL McCARTNEY

MY WAY

Flute

English Words by PAUL ANKA
Original French Words by GILLES THIBAULT
Music by JACQUES REVAUX and CLAUDE FRANCOIS

NANCY WITH THE LAUGHING FACE

Flute

Words by PHIL SILVERS
Music by JAMES VAN HEUSEN

NATURE BOY

FLUTE

Words and Music by
EDEN AHBEZ

NEVER ENOUGH
from THE GREATEST SHOWMAN

Flute

Words and Music by BENJ PASEK
and JUSTIN PAUL

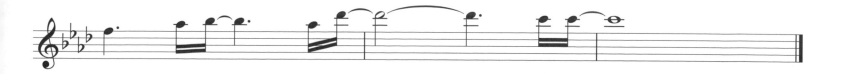

A NIGHTINGALE SANG IN BERKELEY SQUARE

FLUTE

Lyric by ERIC MASCHWITZ
Music by MANNING SHERWIN

PERFECT

FLUTE

Words and Music by
ED SHEERAN

PHOTOGRAPH

Flute

Words and Music by ED SHEERAN,
JOHNNY McDAID, MARTIN PETER HARRINGTON
and TOM LEONARD

(small note optional)

THE PLACE WHERE LOST THINGS GO

from MARY POPPINS RETURNS

FLUTE

Music by MARC SHAIMAN
Lyrics by SCOTT WITTMAN and MARC SHAIMAN

RAINY DAYS AND MONDAYS

Flute

Lyrics by PAUL WILLIAMS
Music by ROGER NICHOLS

Moderately slow

To Coda ⊕ **D.C. al Coda**
(take 2nd ending)

CODA ⊕

RELEASE ME

Flute

Words and Music by ROBERT YOUNT,
EDDIE MILLER and DUB WILLIAMS

REWRITE THE STARS

from THE GREATEST SHOWMAN

Flute

Words and Music by BENJ PASEK
and JUSTIN PAUL

SAILING

FLUTE

Words and Music by
CHRISTOPHER CROSS

SCARBOROUGH FAIR/CANTICLE

FLUTE

Arrangement and Original Counter Melody by
PAUL SIMON and ARTHUR GARFUNKEL

SHALLOW
from A STAR IS BORN

Flute

Words and Music by STEFANI GERMANOTTA,
MARK RONSON, ANDREW WYATT
and ANTHONY ROSSOMANDO

SINCE I DON'T HAVE YOU

Flute

Words and Music by JAMES BEAUMONT,
JANET VOGEL, JOSEPH VERSCHAREN,
WALTER LESTER, LENNIE MARTIN,
JOSEPH ROCK and JOHN TAYLOR

Slowly, with a strong, rockin' beat

SHE'S ALWAYS A WOMAN

FLUTE

Words and Music by
BILLY JOEL

SMILE
Theme from MODERN TIMES

FLUTE

Words by JOHN TURNER and GEOFFREY PARSONS
Music by CHARLES CHAPLIN

SMOKE GETS IN YOUR EYES

from ROBERTA

Flute

Words by OTTO HARBACH
Music by JEROME KERN

Moderately

SOMETHING WONDERFUL

from THE KING AND I

Flute

Lyrics by OSCAR HAMMERSTEIN II
Music by RICHARD RODGERS

SOMEWHERE

from WEST SIDE STORY

Flute

Lyrics by STEPHEN SONDHEIM
Music by LEONARD BERNSTEIN

THE SOUND OF SILENCE

Flute

Words and Music by
PAUL SIMON

STARDUST

Flute

Words by MITCHELL PARISH
Music by HOAGY CARMICHAEL

STRANGERS IN THE NIGHT
adapted from A MAN COULD GET KILLED

Flute

Words by CHARLES SINGLETON
and EDDIE SNYDER
Music by BERT KAEMPFERT

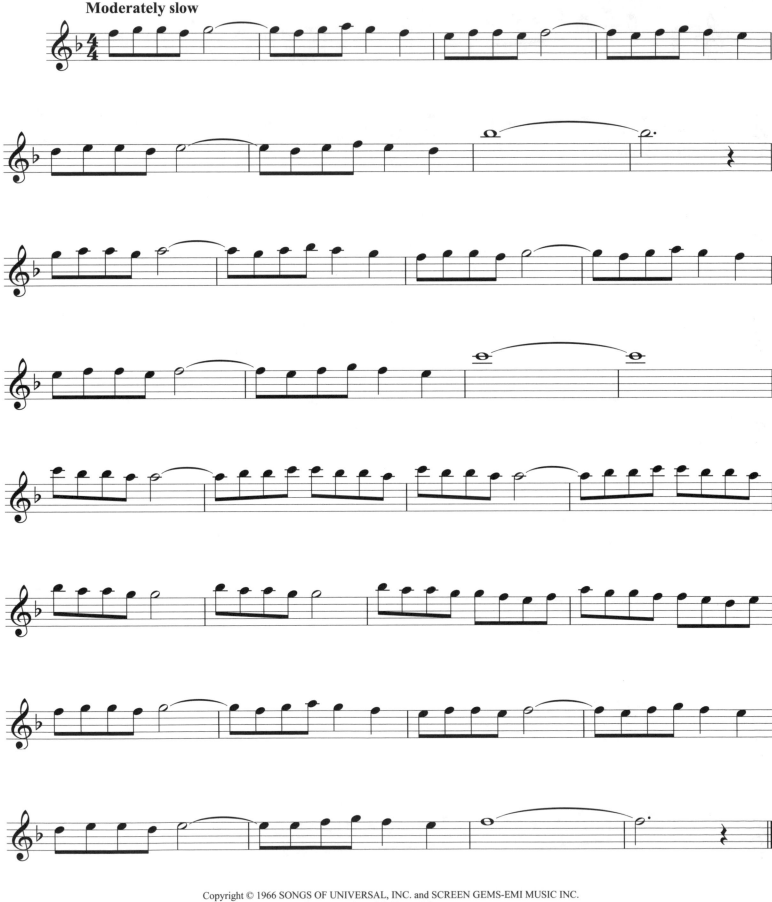

SWAY
(Quien será)

FLUTE

English Words by NORMAN GIMBEL
Spanish Words and Music by PABLO BELTRÁN RUIZ
and LUIS DEMETRIO TRACONIS MOLINA

TENNESSEE WALTZ

Flute

Words and Music by REDD STEWART
and PEE WEE KING

(THERE IS) NO GREATER LOVE

FLUTE

Words by MARTY SYMES
Music by ISHAM JONES

THEY SAY IT'S WONDERFUL

from the Stage Production ANNIE GET YOUR GUN

Flute

Words and Music by
IRVING BERLIN

THREE TIMES A LADY

FLUTE

Words and Music by
LIONEL RICHIE

TIME TO SAY GOODBYE

Flute

Words by LUCIO QUARANTOTTO
and FRANK PETERSON
Music by FRANCESCO SARTORI

(small notes optional)

TRUE COLORS

Flute

Words and Music by BILLY STEINBERG
and TOM KELLY

TRULY

FLUTE

Words and Music by
LIONEL RICHIE

UNEXPECTED SONG
from SONG & DANCE

Music by ANDREW LLOYD WEBBER
Lyrics by DON BLACK

flute

WE'VE ONLY JUST BEGUN

Flute

Words and Music by ROGER NICHOLS
and PAUL WILLIAMS

WE'VE GOT TONIGHT

FLUTE

Words and Music by
BOB SEGER

WHAT A WONDERFUL WORLD

Flute

Words and Music by GEORGE DAVID WEISS
and BOB THIELE

WONDERFUL TONIGHT

FLUTE

Words and Music by
ERIC CLAPTON

YESTER-ME, YESTER-YOU, YESTERDAY

FLUTE

Words by RON MILLER
Music by BRYAN WELLS

YESTERDAY ONCE MORE

Flute

Words and Music by JOHN BETTIS
and RICHARD CARPENTER

YESTERDAY, WHEN I WAS YOUNG
(Hier Encore)

FLUTE

English Lyric by HERBERT KRETZMER
Original French Text and Music by CHARLES AZNAVOUR

YOU ARE THE SUNSHINE OF MY LIFE

FLUTE

Words and Music by
STEVIE WONDER

Moderately

YOU'RE THE INSPIRATION

Flute

Words and Music by PETER CETERA
and DAVID FOSTER

Slow Rock

YOUNG AT HEART

from YOUNG AT HEART

Flute

Words by CAROLYN LEIGH
Music by JOHNNY RICHARDS

YOUR SONG

Flute

Words and Music by ELTON JOHN
and BERNIE TAUPIN